May 1967

RS 3434/8

AEC ATOMIC WEAPON DATA

"HISTORY OF GUN-TYPE

ARTILLERY-FIRED ATOMIC PROJECTILES

Mks 9, 19, 23, 32 and 33 Shells

SC-M-67-659

Weapon Systems

SC-M-67-659
RS-3434/   8
0001A

05/67

Information Research Division, 3434

Redacted Version

THIS DOCUMENT CONSISTS OF 35 PAGES,

2007 0001763

(b)(1), (b)(3)

Mk 9 Shell Cross-Section

RS 3434/8

Mobile Gun Firing Mk 9 Projectile

RS 3434/3

(b)(1), (b)(3)

Mk 19 Shell Cross-Section

RS 3434/8

(b)(1), (b)(3)

MK 33 (T-317)
8" SHELL

TOTAL WT. 243 LBS.

Mk 33 Shell Cross-Section

Timetable of Events

Mk 9 Shell

Late 1949	Army Ordnance proposes development of an artillery-delivered gun-type atomic device.
1/17/50	Los Alamos Scientific Laboratory selects diameter of 280-mm for atomic shell.
5/50	Joint Chiefs of Staff establish military requirement for an artillery-delivered atomic weapon.
6/19/50	Santa Fe Operations Office requests Sandia for design consultation on T124 atomic shell. Button Committee established.
8/11/50	Military characteristics for atomic shell proposed.
10/23/50	Button Committee replaced by TX-9 Committee.
12/18/50	Nomenclature of TX-9 assigned to development of atomic shell.
6/15/51	Quantity production authorized.
1/16/52	TX-9 design released to production.
4/52	Early production of Mk 9 Mod 0 Shell.
7/18/52	Military characteristics released by Military Liaison Committee.
10/14/52	Mk 9 Mod 0 Shell approved for use.
5/23/53	Full-scale test of Mk 9 Mod 0-ZZ Shell in Upshot-Knothole, shot Grable.
11/53	Mk 9 production completed.
4/57	Mk 9 replaced in stockpile by Mk 19 Shell.

Mk 19 Shell

3/53	T315 Shell project established.
6/54	Sandia requested to provide telemetry system for firing tests.
7/55	Early production of Mk 19 Shell.

Mk 23 Shell

12/28/53   Military Liaison Committee forwards development requirement for
            16-inch Navy projectile (Katie) to Division of Military
            Application.

11/1/54   Military characteristics proposed.

7/1/55   Military Liaison Committee approves military characteristics.

10/56   Mk 23 Shell stockpiled.

TX-32 Shell

5/5/54   Division of Military Application requests Santa Fe Operations
            Office to develop a 240-mm atomic shell.

6/18/54   Division of Military Application releases military characteristics
            for T332 Shell.

5/55   Project canceled in favor of XW-48 implosion program.

Mk 33 Shell

6-53   Army Ordnance authorizes development of T317 8-inch atomic
            projectile.

2/54   Development funds for project provided.

4/54   Program placed on crash basis.

2/55   Emergency capability production achieved.

History of Gun-Type Artillery-Fired Atomic Projectiles

Mk 9 Shell

The possibility of developing an artillery-delivered gun-type atomic device was discussed in late 1949 by Army Ordnance. This shell would be a defensive or offensive weapon against infantry masses concentrated in front of the sector through which a breakthrough was planned. It was hoped that a nuclear artillery shell, fuzed for air burst, could destroy the ability of these troops to stage an attack, or to defend the sector.

Possible delivery methods considered for such a weapon included railway rifles, guided missiles, aircraft, or artillery field pieces. Railway rifles, besides being almost obsolate, were ruled out due to heavy weight and relative immobility. Guided missiles capable of carrying atomic warheads were not as yet available. Bombing inaccuracy and difficulty in identifying battlefield targets made use of aircraft-delivered weapons unattractive.

It was felt, however, that artillery field pieces could be used, at least until suitable guided missiles became available. Army Ordnance had developed a mobile gun of 240-mm diameter (about 9-1/2 inches), weighing 90 tons, which was soon to be proof-fired, and a conference was held with Los Alamos Scientific Laboratory personnel November 10, 1949, at which use of this gun was advocated. The nuclear designers stated that a gun-type nuclear device would fit inside a 240-mm gun barrel, although concern was felt about the relatively inefficient usage of fissionable material in such an assembly.[1]

Another meeting was held on the same subject January 16-17, 1950. Increased Los Alamos interest in the project had developed, and Army Ordnance representatives discussed possible shell designs. One proposal was to develop a 240-mm-diameter shell, to fit the mobile gun, and another was to install a 280-mm barrel on the 240-mm mount, thus allowing the shell diameter to increase to about 11 inches.[2]

(b)(1), (b)(3)

It was suggested that Mk 8 internal nuclear components be used. The mobile gun would be test fired in June 1950, and it was hoped that both gun and nuclear shell could become operational at the same time.[3]

Since press of other commitments made it impossible for Los Alamos to participate actively in the project during 1950, it was suggested that the Military assume primary responsibilities for development and testing of the shell. A shock-resistant initiator would be required, and Los Alamos agreed to provide an appropriate design early in 1951.[4]

In May 1950 the Joint Chiefs of Staff established a requirement for the development of an artillery-delivered atomic weapon, and assigned responsibility to Army Ordnance for providing the artillery piece and for developing the nonnuclear parts of the shell.[5] Picatinny Arsenal, Dover, New Jersey, was placed in charge of design work. The shell was given an Army designation of T124, and a schedule was established that called for test firings of scale models in October 1950, full-scale firings in April 1951, and completion of design in April 1952.[6]

The Santa Fe Operations Office requested Sandia, in a letter dated June 19, 1950, to provide any necessary design consultation and to assist in solving problems of storage, surveillance and handling.[7] It was suggested that the project be placed under a committee having representation from Army Ordnance, Los Alamos, Santa Fe Operations Office, and Sandia. The Committee would allocate responsibilities, define weapon characteristics, and generally administer the program.[8] The first meeting of this group, called the Button Coordination Committee, was held July 21, 1950. The shell was variously called T124 Shell,

AFAP (Artillery-Fired Atomic Projectile), and Button (possibly because it was predicted that the shell could be delivered "right on the button").

The Ordnance Department proposed a set of military characteristics that were considered in a Button Committee meeting of August 11, 1950, and accepted on a preliminary basis.[9] The shell would weigh about 890 pounds and be fired with a muzzle velocity of 1700 feet per second from a 280-mm gun mounted on a 240-mm carriage.

(b)(1), (b)(3)

The shell would be able to withstand temperatures from -65°F to +160°F during storage and transportation, and operating-temperature limitations would be determined by the gun itself.[10]

(b)(1), (b)(3)

A device would be designed to provide a surface burst, and it was hoped that this feature could be available concurrently with the time fuze.

The Button Coordination Committee was dissolved October 23, 1950, with Santa Fe Operations Office noting that the number and variety of weapons currently being developed necessitated the establishment of a uniform policy for assignment of responsibilities. Button was in full development but not yet scheduled for production, and Los Alamos and Sandia were requested to assume normal project responsibilities.[12] Subsequently, Sandia took over control of the nonnuclear phases of Button, and reassigned many of the design tasks to Army Ordnance.

(b)(1), (b)(3)

This

UNCLASSIFIED

device had to withstand the shock of firing, and both Picatinny Arsenal and Sandia gave much study to this part of the design.[14]

A TX-G or Gun Committee, with representatives from Los Alamos and Sandia as permanent members, was formed to assume the functions previously carried on by the Button Committee. This committee had cognizance over all gun weapon designs, and initially met December 8, 1950.

(b)(1), (b)(3)

Sandia subsequently assigned nomenclature of TX-9 to the project, December 18, 1950.[16]

The details of the program were then firmed up. Sandia would be responsible for overall nonnuclear development, conduct an evaluation program, certify all nonnuclear parts of the War Reserve shells, establish a training program, supply training shells, and design and procure all nonnuclear assembly and test equipment. The Ordnance Corps would develop War Reserve, training, and spotter shells less nuclear components; design and procure field handling equipment and production tooling; design and procure packaging; and prepare drafts of training literature.[17] Quantity production for the TX-9 was authorized June 15, 1951.[18]

Meanwhile, Picatinny Arsenal had been developing fuze designs.

(b)(1), (b)(3)

UNCLASSIFIED

(b)(1), (b)(3)

However,

subsequent design improvements, selection of high-quality component parts, and eventually, the use of three parallel fuzes, increased operational reliability to the point where timer fuzes were felt to be satisfactory.

Prototype shells were being fired by mid-1951, and demonstrated that nuclear assembly was taking place at the proper point in the trajectory.

(b)(1), (b)(3)

This created a maximum force of 3800 g's. The design of a lighter version with longer range was considered, but the higher stresses involved in this design caused later abandonment of this modification.

(b)(1), (b)(3)

A proposed TX-9 status and characteristics report was prepared by the TX-G Committee. This noted that development of the TX-9 had been telescoped to such an extent that much of the testing would have to be conducted after the design had been released to production.

(b)(1), (b)(3)

Three independently operating mechanical time fuzes were located near the nose of the shell.

(b)(1), (b)(3)

The TX-G Committee met November 2, 1951, and noted that much TX-9 work remained to be done, including testing of the initiators, fuzes, and the conduct of a full-scale nuclear test; and that temperature limitations on both shell and gun were yet to be established. However, the stockpile date would not permit delaying design freeze. There had been no formal issuance of the military characteristics, but the Committee felt that the TX-9 design was adequate for operational use.[22] Design release was accordingly issued November 15, 1951.[23]

The Sandia Weapons Development Board, meeting January 16, 1952, recommended that the TX-9 be released "to" (rather than "for") production.[24] The choice of preposition indicated that the weapon, in some respects such as tests and drawings, was not at the normal stage of release for full production activity.[25] The weapon system was praised for its mobility, and it was noted that the gun could be emplaced in 15 minutes, and that the same length of time was required to assemble and fire the nuclear round.

(b)(1), (b)(3)

The Sandia Weapons Development Board, February 11, 1952, again recommended that the TX-9 be released to production,[26] and this was accepted by the Military Liaison Committee April 14, 1952.[27]

Initial deliveries of the TX-9 to stockpile were made in April 1952, right on schedule. Since the military characteristics had not been issued and the testing program was not completed, these units were temporarily designated as PM-9 or Pre-Mark, rather than by the more formal title of Mk 9 Mod 0.[28]

The military characteristics were officially released by the Military Liaison Committee July 18, 1952.[29]

(b)(1), (b)(3)

(b)(1), (b)(3)

The shell would be able to withstand 100-percent humidity and temperatures up to 90°F.[30]

Sandia recommended to Santa Fe Operations Office October 14, 1952, that the
Mk 9 Mod 0 Shell be approved for operational suitability, training, and emergency use, based on examination of 12 early-production shells from Picatinny
Arsenal. This proposal was accepted, and the first War Reserve-quality shells,
the Mk 9 Mod 0-ZZ, were accepted for stockpiling in October 1952 (ZZ was the
nuclear identification).[31]

(b)(1), (b)(3)

The controllable arming feature of the military characteristics was given atten-
tion. The TX-G Committee took this under consideration, but later noted that
it would be difficult to develop and might degrade the reliability of the shell
due to its complexity.[34] The Committee reported that modification to the Mk 9
Mod 0, to bring it in line with all the military characteristics, would require
much design and testing, and suggested that this work be assigned to the
Ordnance Corps. It was felt that the need for TX-G Committee direction was

declining, and that it could be replaced by an Ad Hoc Committee for each weapon.
On December 15, 1952, the Atomic Energy Commission requested the Military Liaison Committee to transfer responsibility for nonnuclear components of the Mk 9 to the Army, but no action was taken.

The testing program required telemetering of internal events in the Mk 9 Shell, and this posed a difficult problem.

(b)(1), (b)(3)

Sandia had meanwhile concluded that a rugged and accurate telemetering system would be needed for rockets and guided missiles, and started to work on the problem.[36] This was a major undertaking, due to the 5000-g acceleration experienced by the shell. Additionally, the limited space available in the shell case demanded extreme circuit simplicity, and antenna design was severely restricted by the requirement that the external ballistic shape remain unchanged.

Both Army Ordnance and Sandia prepared designs of telemetering systems, and the results were evaluated in a TX-G Committee meeting September 18, 1952. The Ordnance system contained two channels with microsecond time resolution and four with millisecond time resolution. Sandia provided a dual system, each having five channels with microsecond and six with millisecond time resolution.

(b)(1), (b)(3)

The Picatinny system, being immediately available, was used for the first tests, and was later replaced by the Sandia system.[34]

The Sandia telemetering system was tested at Aberdeen in mid-December 1952. Results were generally satisfactory, but swampy terrain prohibited efficient location of telemetering receiving stations, and the range was too short for the maximum range of the Mk 9.[37] A proposal was made that the telemetering tests be conducted at the Nevada Test Site, but the location was later changed

to Ft. Sill, Oklahoma, home of The Artillery Center. These tests were held from
January 19, 1954, to February 5, 1954, with 19 rounds being fired. Telemetering
results were excellent, as was the performance of the Mk 9 Shell.[38]

A full-scale test of the Mk 9 had meanwhile been proposed, both to provide the
Army with an operational test and to allow effects studies both nuclear and
military.[39] A decision was made in late 1952 to conduct this test in Operation
Upshot-Knothole at the Nevada Test Site,[40] and the Mk 9 Mod 0-ZZ Shell was
successfully tested in Shot Grable May 23, 1953.

Some study had been given to updating the stockpiled PM-9's to Mark status.
However, it was felt that the PM-9 was entirely adequate, and that conversion
was not required. Production of the Mk 9 was completed November 1953.

In April 1957, the Mk 9 was replaced in stockpile by the Mk 19 Shell. Mk 9
Shells, tools, and test and handling equipment were transferred to the Army for
training and test purposes.

Mk 19 Shell

By late 1952 it was felt possible to reduce the weight of the Mk 9 Shell by about 200 pounds. This would produce a shell with the same (280-mm or 11-inch) diameter as the Mk 9, but with longer range and higher yield. The proposed atomic projectile would have the same weight as conventional high-explosive 280-mm shells, making it unnecessary to provide special spotting rounds, firing tables, or propellant charges. The Army Ordnance Corps authorized this new project March 1953, and the design of this Shell, called by the Army the T315 or Button II, became the first item of business for the Acorn Committee, which was established April 2, 1953, to centralize work on gun-type weapons.

(b)(1), (b)(3)

                                                        The Division of
Military Application authorized development of this program, called the TX-19 Shell, April 28, 1953.[42]

(b)(1), (b)(3)

Sandia entered the program in June 1954, when the Atomic Energy Commission requested it to provide inflight telemetry for the projectile firing tests.[45] Sandia developed a system by which the internal nuclear events, such as assembly of the subcritical portions of the gun, were monitored.

(b)(1), (b)(3)

The Shell would be 53.62 inches long, about an inch shorter than the Mk 9. The sequence of operation would be identical to the Mk 9, and the two shells would be externally very similar.

(b)(1), (b)(3)

The Army withdrew the requirement for controllable arming. New mechanical fuzes were developed, which were more easily set than those in the Mk 9. Tests were made of an impact device, to determine whether it was safe enough for use, but it did not become available in time.

Stockpiling of the nonnuclear parts of the new weapon started in July 1955.[46] Operational suitability tests were conducted in August 1955, and the Mk 19 was declared satisfactory for field use.   (b)(1), (b)(3)

The increased launching stresses due to the lighter weight required some redesign and strengthening of parts of the ignition, fuzing and safing systems.

The nose fuze and the two internal fuzes of the Mk 19 had redesigned setting features. Settings on the internal fuzes were made with a closed-end ratchet wrench that allowed more rapid and accurate positioning. All fuzes were set in a clockwise direction, facing the nose of the shell, to prevent backlash on firing.[44]

(b)(1), (b)(3)

The Atomic Energy Commission was responsible for development, production and stockpiling of all nuclear components. These were interchangeable between the Mk 8, Mk 9 and Mk 19, and were produced and stockpiled without assignment to any particular weapon

(b)(1), (b)(3)

Mk 23 Shell

The development requirements for a 16-inch atomic projectile were forwarded by the Military Liaison Committee to the Division of Military Application December 28, 1953. These called for the design of a shell to be fired from Naval 16-inch rifles and which would use Mk 19 nuclear components.[47] The project, known as Katie, would develop a shell that could be used for atomic support during amphibious operations.

A design-release date of December 31, 1954, was proposed, with stockpiling by July 1955. The task was a relatively straightforward one; that of adapting the features of the 280-mm T315 (Mk 19) Shell to a case whose external configuration was that of the Navy 16-inch HC Projectile Mk 13.

(b)(1), (b)(3)

Nomenclature of TX-23 was assigned by Sandia March 30, 1954, and was Sandia's only involvement with the project, other than the work being accomplished on the Mk 19, which was also applicable to the Mk 23.[48]

(b)(1), (b)(3)

It was hoped to provide contact cleanup, but on a not-to-delay basis.[50]

The military characteristics were approved by the Military Liaison Committee in mid-1955. The fuzing system would be rugged, reliable, and easily set or reset.

(b)(1), (b)(3)

The shell would function in a temperature range from 0°F to 125°F, and preparation for firing would require no more than 15 minutes.[52] These characteristics were reviewed without comment by Sandia August 15, 1955.[53]

The status of the Mk 23 was discussed in the December 12, 1956 meeting of the Special Weapons Development Board. The shell had a diameter of 16 inches, a length of 63.7 inches, and a weight of 1900 pounds

(b)(1), (b)(3)

The fuzing system contained three independent mechanical time fuzes in the nose of the projectile.

(b)(1), (b)(3)

The Mk 23 was stockpiled, and initial units delivered to the Fleet in October 1956.[54] These initial deliveries were made during the same period that the Navy retired the last 16-inch rifle from active use.

TX-32 Shell

The Division of Military Application, May 5, 1954, requested the Santa Fe
Operations Office to develop a 240-mm (9.45 inch) atomic shell, using the Mk 9
gun-type nuclear components. This design would provide a shell for the Army's
240-mm howitzer. Full-scale development activities were subsequently authorized by the Santa Fe Operations Office, subject to availability of funds and
to orderly integration of the project into the Los Alamos program.[55]

The Military characteristics for a Shell, AE, 240-mm, T332, were released by
the Division of Military Application June 18, 1954. The Army would manage the
project, and the Atomic Energy Commission would furnish nuclear design and
components.[56]

(b)(1), (b)(3)

The design was canceled in May 1955, in favor of an 8-inch
implosion design, the XW-48, which had been proposed by the University of
California Radiation Laboratory.[58]

Mk 33 Shell

In June 1953 the Army Ordnance Corps authorized development of an 8-inch atomic projectile. It was felt that if a shell could be designed that was capable of being fired from a standard mobile field howitzer, it would provide effective fire support for troops and create an important psychological factor in ground warfare.

The Acorn Committee suggested that the design also include consideration of its use in an 8-inch Navy gun.

(b)(1), (b)(3)

Mk 9 nuclear components would be used. [41]

The Army designation was Shell, AE, 8-inch, T317; and the AEC nomenclature was Mk 33. The Army would develop, produce, and stockpile the nonnuclear components, while the Atomic Energy Commission performed the same effort on the nuclear design. The nuclear components were stockpiled without assignment to any particular weapon.

The design remained in the study stage until February 1954, when funds were provided to the Army Ordnance Department for active development work. In April 1954 the Army was requested to have the first production item available for stockpiling by July 1955, and the program was placed on a crash basis.

(b)(1), (b)(3)

The design was made available July 1955, for emergency capability use with the 8-inch howitzer M-2.

(b)(1), (b)(3)

Glossary of Terms

(b)(1), (b)(3)

Field Command -- The local office of the Armed Forces Special Weapon Project, located on Sandia Base, Albuquerque, New Mexico.

g -- Force equal to one unit gravity.

Gun Committee -- A joint committee of Los Alamos Scientific Laboratory and Sandia members, established to guide the development of all gun-type weapons.

Gun-Type Design -- An atomic weapon based on the principle that a supercritical mass of nuclear material can be created by bringing together two subcritical masses of such material. In practice, this is accomplished by placing one of the subcritical masses at the end of a gun barrel and shooting the other subcritical mass into it.

Implosion -- The effect created when a sphere of high explosive is detonated [provided with the appropriate lens charge to direct the explosion] on its exterior surface. The force of the shock wave is directed largely toward the center of the sphere.

Initiator -- A source of neutrons.

Joint Chiefs of Staff -- [A group composed of the Chiefs of Staff of the Army, Navy and Air Force to] determine policy and to develop joint strategic objectives of the Armed Forces.

Kiloton -- A means of measuring the yield of an atomic device by comparing its output with the effect of an explosion of TNT. A 1-kiloton yield is equivalent to the detonation effect of 1000 tons of high explosive.

<u>Los Alamos Scientific Laboratory</u> -- A nuclear design organization located at Los Alamos, New Mexico.

<u>Mk 8 Bomb</u> -- A gun-type atomic bomb and warhead designed for target penetration.

<u>Microsecond</u> -- One millionth of a second.

<u>Military Characteristics</u> -- The attributes of a weapon that are desired by the Military.

<u>Military Liaison Committee</u> -- A Department of Defense committee established by the Atomic Energy Act to advise and consult with the AEC on all matters relating to military applications of atomic energy.

<u>Millisecond</u> -- One thousandth of a second.

<u>Operation Buster-Jangle</u> -- See Buster-Jangle.

<u>Operation Upshot-Knothole</u> -- See Upshot-Knothole.

<u>Oralloy</u> -- A code term for enriched uranium. The two initial letters stand for <u>Oak Ridge</u> (where Oralloy was first made in quantity) added to <u>alloy</u> from Tube Alloys, Ltd., applied to the British wartime atomic energy project.

<u>Picatinny Arsenal</u> -- An arsenal of the Army, responsible for design of nuclear weapons for the Army.

<u>Prototype</u> -- An early weapon type, generally hand-produced before a production run.

<u>Proximity Fuze</u> -- A fuze that detonates the weapon as soon as it comes within a certain specified distance of the ground or target.

<u>Sandia Weapons Development Board</u> -- A joint Sandia-Military board at Sandia Base to provide local guidance on weapons design.

<u>Santa Fe Operations Office</u> -- The local office of the Atomic Energy Commission (AEC) concerned with Sandia operations.

<u>Special Weapons Development Board</u> -- Change of name for the Sandia Weapons Development Board, effective May 14, 1952.

<u>Spotter Shells</u> -- Nonnuclear shells that contain the same weight of projectile and powder charge as the atomic Shell. Can be used for proper range determination before the nuclear shell is fired.

(b)(1), (b)(3)

<u>University of California Radiation Laboratory</u> -- A laboratory established at Livermore, California. Initially founded for work on thermonuclear designs.

<u>Upshot-Knothole</u> -- Tests of atomic devices, held at the Nevada Test Site. Series of 11 shots, starting March 17 and ending June 4, 1953.

<u>Uranium-235</u> -- A radioactive element, an isotope of uranium-238.

<u>Uranium-238</u> -- A radioactive element, atomic number 92. Natural uranium contains about 99.3-percent of uranium-238; the rest is uranium-235.

<u>Yield</u> -- ~~A means of measuring~~ The measure of the effect of a nuclear detonation ~~by comparing it with~~ compared to the effect of an explosion of TNT. By definition one kiloton is 10^{12} calories.

1. SRD Ltr, Los Alamos Scientific Laboratory to Distribution, dtd 11/10/49, subject, Notes of Meeting by George B. Sabine, W-4. AEC Files, Organization and Management, 7/49-12/49.

2. SRD Ltr, Los Alamos Scientific Laboratory to Army Ordnance, dtd 1/31/50. AEC Files, MRA, Mk 9, 1/50-6/50.

3. SRD Ltr, Armed Forces Special Weapons Project, Washington, D. C., to Division of Military Application, dtd 1/31/50, subject, Gun-Fired Atomic Weapon. AEC Files, MRA, Mk 9, 1/50-6/50.

4. SRD Ltr, Los Alamos Scientific Laboratory to Santa Fe Operations Office, dtd 3/15/50, subject, Gun-Type Atomic Weapon. AEC Files, MRA, Mk 9, 1/50-6/50.

5. SRD Ltr, RS 3421-4/2430, U. S. Atomic Energy Commission to Army Ordnance, dtd 5/15/50, subject, Artillery Delivered Atomic Weapon. SC Archives, microfilm reel MF-SF-SC-29.

6. SRD Ltr, Army Ordnance Department to U. S. Atomic Energy Commission, dtd 5/17/50, subject, Artillery Delivered Atomic Weapon. AEC Files, MRA, Mk 9, 1/50-6/50.

7. SRD Ltr, Santa Fe Operations Office to AEC-Sandia, dtd 6/19/50, subject, Artillery Fired Atomic Projectile. AEC Files, MRA, 9-1, TX-9, 5/50-3/51.

8. SRD Ltr, RS 3421-4/1426, Santa Fe Operations Office to Army Ordnance, dtd 6/19/50. SC Archives, microfilm reel MF-SF-SC-29.

9. SRD Minutes, Button Coordination Committee to Distribution, dtd 7/21/50, subject, Minutes of 1st Meeting. SC Archives, TX-9, 1-7, Transfer No. 29891.

10. SRD Minutes, RS 3421-4/2432, Button Coordination Committee to Distribution, dtd 8/11/50, subject, Minutes of 2nd Meeting. SC Archives, microfilm reel MF-SF-SC-43.

11.

(b)(3)

12. CRD Ltr, Santa Fe Operations Office to Army Ordnance, dtd 10/23/50, subject, Project Button. SC Archives, TX-9, 1-3, Transfer No. 29748.

13.

(b)(3)

14. SRD Ltr, Los Alamos Scientific Laboratory to Santa Fe Operations Office, dtd 12/8/50, subject, Scope of Ordnance Corps Work on Project Button. AEC Files, MRA-5, Mk 9, 9/50-12/50.

15.

(b)(3)

16. SRD Ltr, Sandia Corporation to Distribution, dtd 1/4/51, subject, TX-9 (Button) Progress Report--Fourth Quarter Calendar 1950. AEC Files, Mk 9, 1/51-3/51.

17. SRD Ltr, RS 1/123, Sandia Corporation to Santa Fe Operations Office, dtd 6/4/51, subject, TX-9 Development Program. SC Archives, microfilm reel MF-SF-SC-47.

18. SRD Ltr, Santa Fe Operations Office to Sandia Corporation, Los Alamos Scientific Laboratory and AEC-Sandia, dtd 6/15/51, subject, TX-9 and Mk 9 Scheduling. AEC Files, MRA, 9-1, TX-9, 4/51-7/51.

19.

20.

(b)(3)

21.

22. SRD Minutes, RS 3466/60892, TX-G Committee to Distribution, dtd 11/2/51, subject, Minutes of 12th Meeting. SC Reports Files.

23. SRD Report, RS 1230/39, Sandia Corporation to Distribution, dtd 3/11/52, subject, Development Status, Mk 9 Weapon. AEC Files, MRA, Mk 9, 3/52-4/52.

24. SRD Minutes, RS 3466/60958, Sandia Weapons Development Board to Distribution, dtd 1/16/52, subject, Minutes of 59th Meeting. SC Archives, Transfer No. 48217.

25. SRD Ltr, RS 1/211, Sandia Corporation to Los Alamos Scientific Laboratory, dtd 1/9/52, subject, TX-9. Forms Appendix I to TK-G Steering Committee Minutes, 14th Meeting, 1/17/52, RS 3466/61369. SC Reports Files.

26. SRD Ltr, RS 1/228, Sandia Corporation to Division of Military Application, dtd 2/11/52. AEC Files, MRA, Mk 9, 2/52.

27. SRD Ltr, Military Liaison Committee to Division of Military Application, dtd 4/14/52, subject, Release to Production TX-9. AEC Files, 9-1, TX-9, 4/52-5/52.

28. SRD Ltr, Santa Fe Operations Office to Division of Military Application, dtd 6/19/52, subject, Stockpile Entry of TX-9 Weapon. Forms Appendix II to TX-G Steering Committee Minutes, 6/19/52. SC Reports Files.

29. SRD Ltr, Military Liaison Committee to Division of Military Application, dtd 7/18/52, subject, Military Characteristics for Shell, 280-mm, Atomic. SC Archives, Mk 9, Transfer No. 31366-7.

30. SRD Ltr, Santa Fe Operations Office to Los Alamos Scientific Laboratory and Sandia Corporation, dtd 8/15/52. SC Archives, TX-9, 1-9, Transfer No. 29891.

31. SRD Ltr, Santa Fe Operations Office to Division of Military Application, dtd 10/30/52, subject, First Approval of Mk 9 Mod 0 Weapon for Operational Suitability, Training and Emergency Use. AEC Files, MRA, Mk 9. 1/52-12/52.

32.

33.   (b)(3)

34. SRD Minutes, RS 3466/67384, TX-G Steering Committee to Distribution, dtd 9/18/52, subject, Minutes of 21st Meeting. SC Reports Files.

35.
                                                       (b)(3)

36. SRD Ltr, RS 5000/22, Sandia Corporation to Santa Fe Operations Office, dtd 5/29/52, subject, Tests of the TX-9 Telemetering System. AEC Files, MRA, Mk 9, 5/52-6/52.

37. SRD Ltr, RS 1/411, Sandia Corporation to Field Command, dtd 12/15/52, subject, Firing of Mk 9 Telemetering Test Round. AEC Files, MRA, Mk 9, 1/52-12/52.

38. SRD Report, RS 5222/28, Division 5222 to Distribution, dtd 3/11/54, subject, Operational Field Notes on Test of Mk 9 Weapon at Fort Sill, Oklahoma. SC Archives, TX-9, 3-1, 1953-4, Transfer No. 29890.

39. SRD Ltr, RS 1/317, Sandia Corporation to Santa Fe Operations Office, dtd 7/8/52, subject, Full Scale Test of the Atomic Shell. AEC Files, MRA, Mk 9, 1/52-12/52.

40. SRD Ltr, U. S. Atomic Energy Commission to Secretary of Defense, dtd 11/17/52. AEC Files, MRA, Mk 9, 1/52-12/52.

41.   (b)(3)

42. SRD Ltr, Santa Fe Operations Office to Los Alamos Scientific Laboratory, dtd 5/5/53, subject, 280-mm Atomic Shell with Longer Range. AEC Files, MRA, 9-1, TX-9, 4/54.

43.
                                          (b)(3)

44.

45. SRD Ltr, AEC-Sandia to Sandia Corporation, dtd 6/18/54, subject, Request for Feasibility Study. AEC Files, MRA-5.

46.
                                          (b)(3)

47.

48. SRD Ltr, RS 1000/1526, Sandia Corporation to AEC-Sandia, dtd 3/30/54, subject, Assignment of TX-23 Designation. AEC Files, MRA-5, Mk 23.

49.   (b)(1), (b)(3)

50. SRD Report, TX-N Committee to Distribution, dtd 11/8/54, subject, Guided Missiles Status Report. SC Central Technical Files, C-6.

51.   (b)(1), (b)(3)

52. SRD Ltr, RS 3466/87562, Santa Fe Operations Office to Sandia Corporation,
     dtd 7/11/55, subject, Military Characteristics of the 16-Inch Projectile
     Mk 23 Mod 0. SC Archives, M23 and TX-23.

53. SRD Ltr, RS 1300/509, Sandia Corporation to Santa Fe Operations Office,
     dtd 8/15/55, subject, Military Characteristics for the 16-Inch Projectile
     Mk 23 Mod 0. AEC Files, MRA-5, Mk 23.

54. SRD Minutes, RS 3466/82347, Special Weapons Development Board to Distribu-
     tion, dtd 12/12/56, subject, Minutes of 104th Meeting, Part I. SC Archives,
     Transfer No. 48217.

55. SRD Ltr, RS 3466/139318, Santa Fe Operations Office to Los Alamos Scientific
     Laboratory, dtd 5/24/54, subject, Development Program for 240-mm Atomic
     Shell. SC Archives, Mk 9, Transfer No. 31366-7.

56. SRD Ltr, RS 3466/139320, Division of Military Application to Santa Fe Oper-
     ations Office, dtd 6/18/54, subject, Military Characteristics for 240-mm
     Atomic Shell. SC Archives, Mk 9, Transfer No. 31366-7.

57.   (b)(3)

58. SRD Ltr, RS 3466/72885, Military Liaison Committee to U. S. Atomic Energy
     Commission, dtd 9/9/55, subject, Suspension of 240-mm Shell Program. SC
     Central Technical Files, TX-32, 1955.